SERVING YOUR COMMUNITY

A TRUE BOOK®

by
Christin Ditchfield

Children's Press®
A Division of Scholastic Inc.

New York Toronto London Auckland Sydney
Mexico City New Delhi Hong Kong
Danbury, Connecticut

An older student
helping a
younger student

Reading Consultant
Jeanne Clidas, Ph.D.
*National Reading Consultant
and Professor of Reading,
SUNY Brockport*

Library of Congress Cataloging-in-Publication Data

Ditchfield, Christin.
  Serving your community / by Christin Ditchfield.
      p. cm. — (A true book)
Includes bibliographical references and index.
Contents: Calling all volunteers—Serving people—Saving the planet—
Solving problems—Doing your part.
  ISBN 0-516-22802-1 (lib. bdg.)   0-516-27911-4 (pbk.)
  1. Voluntarism—Juvenile literature. [1. Voluntarism.] I. Title. II. Series.
HN49.V64 D57 2003
361.3'7—dc21
                                                              2003005176

CHILDREN'S PRESS, and A TRUE BOOK™, and associated logos are
trademarks and or registered trademarks of Scholastic Library Publishing.
SCHOLASTIC and associated logos are trademarks and or registered
trademarks of Scholastic Inc.
  3 4 5 6 7 8 9 10 R 13 12 11 10 09 08 07 06

Contents

These kids are painting a mural to help beautify their neighborhood.

Calling All Volunteers

On January 20, 1961, John F. Kennedy became the thirty-fifth president of the United States. In a famous speech, President Kennedy called on all Americans to work together to make their nation a better place to live.

Kennedy said, "Ask not what your country can do for you—ask what you can do for your country."

President Kennedy called on all Americans to help make the world a better place.

The president reminded
people that citizens of the
United States have many
privileges and freedoms.
They also have responsibilities.

Good citizens work to strengthen their families, neighborhoods, and communities.

Every day across the country, millions of people volunteer. They give their time and effort to help others in their communities. They share their **resources** with people in need. They care for animals and wildlife. They protect the **environment**. These people work to make their neighborhoods cleaner, safer, and more pleasant to live in.

Volunteers at an animal shelter

People cleaning up litter
in their neighborhood

They speak out about issues that are important to them. They don't just complain about problems—they look for ways to solve them!

People who volunteer do not get paid for their work. They do it because they care. Volunteers know that by working together, they can make a difference in our world.

Serving People

Many people choose to volunteer by helping other people. Some volunteers help people with physical needs. They assist elderly or dis-abled people by doing yard work and housecleaning for them. They may drive them to doctor appointments or

religious services. They deliver
hot meals or help them go
grocery shopping.

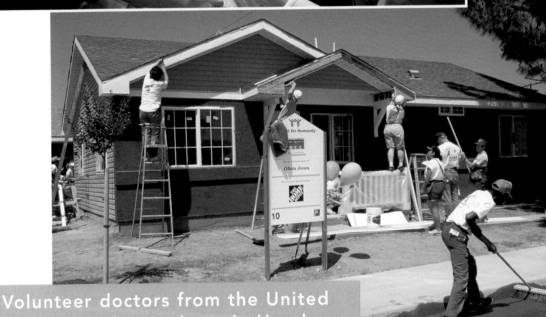

Volunteer doctors from the United States treating patients in Honduras (top) and volunteers building a home for a person who could not otherwise afford one (bottom)

Volunteer doctors and nurses travel to remote areas to provide medical treatment to those who live there. Other volunteers work with community groups to build homes for people who could not otherwise afford them. They collect food for the hungry. They create shelters for the homeless—those who live on the street.

Some people train helper dogs to assist people who are blind or deaf. Others

Foster parents are people who open their homes to children who need families.

open their homes to children who have no families to take care of them.

Volunteers also help people with educational needs. They teach people skills that will help them find better jobs. Literacy volunteers work with adults who want to learn how to read. Tutors study with children who are struggling in school. They give them extra help with their homework.

Sometimes volunteers who have special training will offer to assist people with compli-cated tasks. They may help them learn to use computers, make minor car or home repairs, or help them file their tax returns. Others teach

A volunteer (left) teaches English to a woman from Colombia (right).

English to people who have come to the United States from other countries.

Volunteers help people with emotional needs. They provide friendship, comfort, and encouragement. They visit sick

people in the hospital to cheer them up. They spend time with people who are alone or are far away from friends or family. **Counselors** listen to people who have problems and try to help them find solutions.

When Times are Tough

Sometimes terrible things happen to people. They may get hurt or injured. Their homes may be destroyed by flood or fire, leaving them with no place to live. If people lose their jobs, they may not be able to afford food and clothing.

In tough times, it is especially important for volunteers to help those who cannot help themselves. Volunteers make it possible for individuals and communities to recover and rebuild their lives.

These photos show volunteers helping out during a flood.

Saving the Planet

Many people volunteer to protect and preserve the environment. They care about nature. They want to keep the planet healthy.

Volunteers talk to community groups about the importance of preserving Earth's natural resources. They remind people

A volunteer giving out information about recycling

ONLY
WHITE
OFFICE PAPER
PLEASE!

Kids recycling

to conserve water and energy. They plant trees to replace those that have been cut down for use in construction or to make paper products.

Volunteers also create programs to encourage people to recycle and reuse products instead of sending everything to garbage dumps. Some families collect dead leaves and plants and kitchen scraps in containers. These materials then rot and form a type of

Volunteers working on a community garden

fertilizer called compost,
which can be used to enrich
the soil. Others plant gardens

and grow fruits and vegetables
for themselves or for distribu-
tion to the needy.

Volunteers sign **petitions**
and promote laws that prevent
pollution. They work to keep
factories from dumping dan-
gerous chemicals into the air,
water, or soil.

Volunteers also promote
laws that protect animals from
inhumane, or cruel, treatment.
They provide shelters to care
for pets that have been lost,

abandoned, or neglected. They rescue animals that are hurt or injured.

Some people volunteer to raise awareness of **endangered** species. They seek to protect animals and animal **habitats** that are in danger of being destroyed.

Many people forget about their natural environment. They don't think about the things they do that could damage Earth or its creatures. Some

A wildlife-center volunteer taking care of an injured great blue heron

volunteers try to teach people the importance of caring for wildlife and natural resources.

Solving Problems

Some people volunteer to try to solve problems. They speak out about issues that concern them and their families. They see a need in their community and they take action to get that need met. They work to find solutions that will help everyone live better lives.

People speaking out against air pollution

A young person taking part in a bike-safety course

Many volunteers are concerned about safety. They teach bicycle safety and help children learn the rules of the road. They encourage families to check their smoke detectors and prepare an escape plan in case of a fire. In some communities, the firefighters themselves are all volunteers.

Volunteers remind people to wear seat belts and drive safely. They work to make traffic lights and road signs more visible. They ask cities to put in more sidewalks, bicycle lanes, and streetlights. Volunteers organize neighbor-hood watch groups to prevent crime by reporting **suspicious** activity to the police.

Other volunteers are concerned about health issues. Groups offer free hearing and vision tests for the elderly and for elementary-school students. Volunteers give speeches to teach people about proper **nutrition**. They teach disease prevention and raise money for medical research. They organize exercise classes. Volunteers visit schools to warn young people about the dangers of smoking and drug use.

A volunteer from a medical clinic gives a presentation in Spanish about how to stay healthy.

Others remind them of the awful **consequences** of alcohol abuse and drunk driving.

Doing Your Part

There are many ways you can serve your community. You can reach out to people in your neighborhood, work to solve problems, or take steps to help save the environment. You can raise money to support a cause or raise awareness about a particular issue.

People participating in a car wash to raise money for the homeless

Planting a tree is one way to contribute to your community.

You can take action physically by picking up trash or planting a tree. You can take action politically by contacting government officials and promoting laws that preserve or protect something that is important to you. Every area has civic clubs, community groups, and religious organizations that work together to connect volunteers with opportunities to serve.

It's true that no one person can solve all of the world's problems. No one person can meet every need. But one person can do one thing. One person can support one cause. One person can make a big difference simply by volunteering whatever time, energy, skills, or resources he or she has. One person can join another person and another and another. People can combine their efforts, working together to serve their community and make the world a better place.

Many communities have programs in which older kids volunteer to be "big brothers" or "big sisters" to younger kids.

You don't have to be an adult to volunteer. There are many ways kids can make a difference in their communities. Here are just a few ideas:

- Draw a poster about bicycle safety.

- Start a food drive to help collect canned goods for the needy.

- Do yard work for an elderly neighbor.

Help a younger child with his or her homework.

Practice fire-safety drills with your family.

Clean up litter in and around your school.

Make holiday cards for children in the hospital.

Build a bird feeder or butterfly garden in your backyard.

Remind friends and family to recycle.

Write a letter to the editor of your local newspaper about an issue you care about.

To Find Out More

Here are some additional resources to help you learn more about serving your community:

 **Books**

Erlbach, Arlene. **The Kids' Volunteering Book.** Lerner Publications Company, 2003.

Isler, Claudia. **Volunteering to Help in Your Neighborhood.** Children's Press, 2000.

Lewis, Barbara A. **The Kid's Guide to Service Projects.** Free Spirit Publishing, Inc., 1995.

Mintzer, Richard. **Helping Hands: How Families Can Reach Out to Their Community.** Chelsea House Publishers, 2002.

Wandburg, Robert. **Volunteering: Giving Back.** Capstone Press, 2001.

Organizations and Online Sites

American Red Cross
431 18th Street NW
Washington, DC 20006
http://www.redcross.org

With the help of more than a million volunteers, the Red Cross provides emergency assistance and disaster relief to needy people around the world.

National Safety Council
1121 Spring Lake Drive
Itasca, IL 60143
http://www.nsc.org

This site provides information and education programs to "protect life and promote health."

United States Environmental Protection Agency Environmental Explorer's Club
http://www.epa.gov/kids/

This site combines facts with fun by offering games, contests, and ways you can help protect the environment.

Youth Service America
1101 15th Street, Suite 200
Washington, DC 20005
http://www.ysa.org

This group organizes and develops volunteer opportunities for young people to serve locally, nationally, and globally.

Important Words

consequences results of an action

counselors people trained to give advice

endangered in danger of dying out

environment one's natural surroundings

habitats places where plants or animals naturally live

nutrition act or process of taking in foods that keep one healthy

petitions letters signed by many people demanding change

privileges special advantages

resources things that are valuable

suspicious something that appears wrong or bad

Index

Meet the Author

Christin Ditchfield is an author and conference speaker, and is host of the nationally syndicated radio program *Take It to Heart!* Her articles have been featured in magazines all over the world. A former elementary-school teacher, Christin has written more than twenty-five books for children on a wide range of topics, including sports, science, and history. She makes her home in Sarasota, Florida.